IMAGES
*of America*

# HANOVER HARVESTERS

A PICTORIAL HISTORY OF
HANOVER TOWNSHIP 1850–1955

IMAGES
*of America*

# HANOVER HARVESTERS

## A PICTORIAL HISTORY OF HANOVER TOWNSHIP 1850–1955

Nancy Gher and Jennifer Leo

ARCADIA

ISBN 0-7385-0021-6

Published by Arcadia Publishing,
an imprint of Tempus Publishing, Inc.
2 Cumberland Street
Charleston, SC 29401

Printed in Great Britain.

Library of Congress Catalog Card Number applied for.

For all general information contact Arcadia Publishing at:
Telephone 843-853-2070
Fax 843-853-0044
E-Mail arcadia@charleston.net

For customer service and orders:
Toll-Free 1-888-313-BOOK

Visit us on the internet at http://www.arcadiaimages.com

# Contents

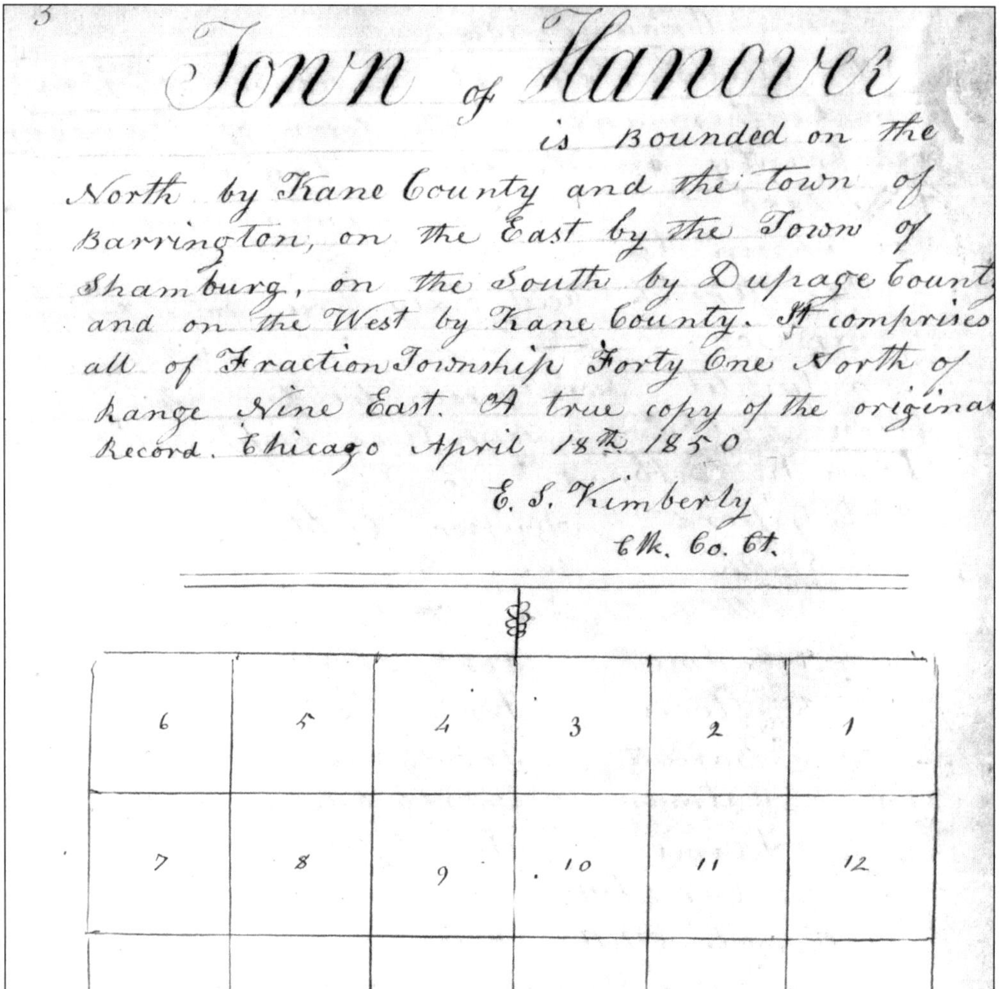
Town of Hanover is Bounded on the North by Kane County and the town of Barrington, on the East by the Town of Shamburg, on the South by Dupage County and on the West by Kane County. It comprises all of Fraction Township Forty One North of Range Nine East. A true copy of the original Record. Chicago April 18th 1850

E. S. Kimberly
Clk. Co. Ct.

| 6 | 5 | 4 | 3 | 2 | 1 |
|---|---|---|---|---|---|
| 7 | 8 | 9 | 10 | 11 | 12 |
| 18 | 17 | 16 | 15 | 14 | 13 |
| 19 | 20 | 21 | 22 | 23 | 24 |
| 30 | 29 | 28 | 27 | 26 | 25 |
| 31 | 32 | 33 | 34 | 35 | 36 |

This hand-drawn plat of Hanover Township was created on April 18, 1950.

# INTRODUCTION

April 2, 1850, was in many ways an ordinary day for the farm families of far northwestern Cook County, Illinois. There was spring planting to finish. Cows needed milking, chickens needed feeding, and farm implements needed to be cleaned and oiled after the long winter. But sometime during that day, the farmers took a break from their chores to gather at Abraham Leatherman's tavern. There, they held the first election in the newly formed township called Hanover.

Less than 20 years earlier, the first non-native settlers had set up housekeeping in the area. Before that, the land was home to Native Americans: first the Miami, Shawnee, Fox, Sauk, and Illinois; later the Ottawa and Ojibwa; and, finally, the Potawatomi.

The year 1832 brought the Blackhawk War and with it, and soldiers marched from their base in Chicago to the battlefields near the Rock River valley. With the signing of the Treaty of Chicago in 1832, the Potowatomi reluctantly gave up their land in northern Illinois and were removed to reservations in Kansas and Iowa. By the mid-1830s, streams of immigrants and Easterners poured into the newly available land, lured by reports of rich soil, abundant virgin timber, and the growing marketplace in nearby Chicago. Some passed through on their way to stake claims further west. Others remained and set up farms in what would become Hanover Township.

The early settlers arrived in 1835 to farm the rich Midwestern soil. Most of them were Americans of English descent, either New England "Yankees" or "Yorkers," who hailed from New York State. One exception was a group from Indiana—hence the name "Hoosier Grove," the predecessor to Streamwood.

In 1850, the first federal census of Hanover Township reported a population of 672 and growing. Farmers delivering their wheat crop to Chicago by wagon, over rough roads, brought a steady stream of new settlers back with them on the return trip.

The next census in 1860 accounted for 926 residents. By then, a change had occurred in the composition of the Hanover population. Foreign-born heads of households now outnumbered the Yankees, Yorkers, and Hoosiers. By 1870, 46% of

Hanover Township's 1,098 residents were mostly German-born foreigners. Political upheaval in their homeland and the promise of freedom in the U.S., combined with a desire to farm, attracted large numbers of Germans to the area, which they called Hanover after their native region.

Looking over the landscape of Hanover Township today, it's hard to imagine how it must have looked 150 years ago. Where we see well-kept lawns, the farmer of 1850 saw prairie grass and acres of corn and wheat. Where we drive smoothly on heavily trafficked streets, the farmer broke wagon wheels on deeply rutted roads that had been Potawatomi trails not long before. The general store has given way to the strip mall—the threshing picnic to the fast-food lunch. There are fewer and fewer traces of the way life used to be.

This book is not meant to be a scholarly history of Hanover Township. It is reminiscence, a walk down memory lane, and a slice of life from an era that's slipping father into the past—the era of pre-suburban farm life in Hanover Township. As we blaze a new trail into the 21st century, let's take a look back to see how far we've come. *Hanover Harvesters* is an attempt to preserve a small portion of the lives of ordinary citizens who spent their days in Hanover Township when it was a thriving agricultural community.

Most of the subject matter in this pictorial history dates from 1880 to 1955, since those were the years for which the most photographic records are available. We remember, however, that the true history of Hanover Township extends back to that first meeting in Leatherman's tavern, and also stretches forward to those who live, work, and play in Hanover Township in the 21st century. They, too, are quietly making history every day.

# *One*

# Working the Land

The Hecht farm, shown here *c.* 1895, was located on Irving Park Road near what is now Nana's Restaurant. In the mid-1800s, the Hanover area led Cook County in wheat production. However, over time the fertile soil was depleted and wheat was no longer the principal source of income. The growing population of Chicago created a greater demand for dairy products. These factors, coupled with the arrival of the railroad, influenced local farmers to convert to dairy farming.

A good healthy herd of cows made a dairy farmer proud. Here, the Heine children and friends admire the family cows, c. 1912.

This photograph shows Louis Struckmeier and his grandchildren in the early 1900s. The Struckmeiers moved to Hanover after their home was destroyed in the Great Chicago Fire of 1871. The Struckmeier farm was located at what is now Hoosier Grove Park. Today, the country road in the background is busy Irving Park Road.

Moving cows to and from pasture was a twice-daily chore. This herd belonged to the Voss family, who later owned the Struckmeier farm. The herd is shown crossing Irving Park Road in the 1940s.

Occasionally, children treated cows as pets (to the consternation of their parents). Here, the Heine children and friends enjoy a cow-back ride, *c*. 1912.

Hanover area children display blue ribbons won at a milking competition, *c.* 1920.

Students from Helberg School show off banners they won in a milking contest at the Bartlett School Festival, June 5, 1924. Milking was a highly valued skill on Hanover farms.

On the Struckmeier farm, *c.* 1895, a wagon is loaded for a trip to market. Milk in cans was carried by wagon to nearby creameries for processing or to the Bartlett or Ontarioville depots for shipment to Chicago. Later, the railroads sent trucks to pick up the milk at the farms.

Hanover creameries provided a local market for farmers' milk. Several operated in the area, including one built in 1868 behind the August Nolting farm. German immigrant August Nolting owned half interest in this creamery, which was located on North Bartlett Road, south of the present location of Route 58. The stacks seen in the background mark the location of the creamery.

Both built in 1873, the train stations at Ontarioville and Bartlett were hubs of activity. After loading their milk onto the trains, farmers might stop at the bank, the general store, and perhaps the tavern for a quick refreshment and a bit of socializing before heading home.

This photograph shows the interior of Bartlett's Huntley Dairy. The men include Peter Butz, Ed Waterman and Bill Jackle; the fourth is unknown.

Some milk was processed at local dairies and creameries such as the Huntley Dairy in Bartlett, located on Main Street just south of the railroad tracks.

This creamery was located in Ontarioville. The manager also owned a cheese factory; he lived in a house right between the two operations.

A conveyor belt moves cans of milk in the processing plant of the Huntley Dairy Co. in Bartlett, *c*. 1909.

The process of threshing, separating grains from the chaff, can be seen in the image above. The introduction of the steam-powered thresher was a great boon to farm work. This photograph shows the Hecht threshing gang at work on the Heine farm, *c.* 1918.

The Hechts display the steam-powered engine used for threshing, *c.* 1900. Fred Hecht Jr. stands by the engine while Fred Hecht Sr. is behind the wheel. The men in the background are the threshing crew, hired in season to help with the enormous amount of work. Threshing crews, or "gangs," would move from farm to farm as each field was threshed. The Hecht family ran a threshing business in rural Hanover for over 40 years.

Fred Hecht Jr., his family, and friends pose proudly with a brand-new Buffalo-Pitts 35-horsepower twin-cylinder steam engine—the high-tech farm implement of its day. The steam engine was used for many farm chores, from threshing to filling the silo with silage.

New technology did not always run smoothly. Old-fashioned horsepower was needed on the Heine farm to pull a new-fangled tractor out of the mud.

Tall haystacks were a familiar sight on Hanover farms. Hay was tossed into a stack using pitchforks. The Heine children and friends posed for this photograph *c.* 1918.

Later advances in technology made it possible to replace haystacks with neat bales of hay. This 1940s photograph shows a steam-powered baler in use on the Blume farm, which was located on Route 19 near where the Jewel/Osco store now stands. Seen above, from left to right, are Irvin Pflug, Herbert Blume, Harold Blume, and Vernon Blume.

Amanda Hecht rolls out dough for biscuits. Hanover women prepared meals not only for their families, but for hired farmhands, too.

"Women's work" on the farm was arduous and physical. In addition to cooking and caring for the home and children, women worked in the fields, cared for animals, gardened, canned, and took goods to market. One of the regular chores for women on the farm was making pickles.

Laundry was an ever-present chore, both winter and summer, as is demonstrated by this hard-working woman on the Hecht farm.

Caring for children was a primary activity for farm women. Multiple generations often lived under the same roof or nearby, allowing for lots of interaction between grandparents and grandchildren. Here, Florence Lamprecht takes a walk with her grandmother.

Farm women needed to be strong to harvest crops in the fields. This image was taken at the Tatge farm, *c*. 1915.

Planting, plowing, and handling a strong team of horses were women's work when help was needed in the fields, as can be seen in this *c.* 1915 photograph taken at the Tatge farm.

Tending horses, pigs, chickens, and other animals was an important part of the farm women's day. This photograph shows Mary Heine leading her horse, Maud, *c.* 1915.

A Hanover woman tends her chickens on the Tatge farm, *c.* 1915.

These women are caring for chicks on the Hecht farm, *c*. 1918.

Women raised chickens and sold the birds and eggs for pocket change. Chicks could be purchased from hatcheries in Ontarioville and Elgin, or via mail order through ads such as these, which appeared in the *Kane County Farmer* in 1935.

Cows were not the only animals raised by Hanover farmers. Sheep were raised for wool as well as meat. This device on the Hecht farm was a stand used for bagging wool on shearing days. A large canvas bag would be suspended from the top of the stand and filled with wool.

Sheep graze at the Flentge farm, *c.* 1915.

Hogs were raised for their meat and were used mostly for family consumption. Fred Hecht poses here with two fine specimens.

This photograph shows Mary Heine caring for an impressive flock of geese, which were valued for their meat and feathers, *c.* 1915. The Heine flock included up to 70 or 80 geese at a time.

Butchering pigs and hogs was primarily a late fall activity. This 1919 image was taken at the Heine farm.

The slaughtered hog is hung from a tree, as can be seen in this *c.* 1928 image of the Krog farm. The next stop is the smokehouse.

A worker on the Heine farm proudly displays a slaughtered pig that will help feed the family through the long winter.

Goose slaughtering appears to be a community activity at the Heine farm.

Farm children were expected to help with chores from an early age. Mildred Heine and Esther Harz take a break from working in the field to mug for the camera, while Mildred's father waits patiently in the background.

Horses were important animals on Hanover farms, both for transportation and for field work. Teams of horses were used on the farm well into the 1930s. Here, Art Heine shows his nephews, Orville and Donald Pelletier, the ropes of handling a team of horses.

Caring for pets and small animals prepared children to help with the larger livestock. This photograph shows Ralph Heine and his puppies.

Art Heine, age 13, cares for a baby pig. The pig was "one too many" from a litter of a neighbor, who gave the pig to Art to nurse and raise.

Most Hanover farmers began to convert to beans and corn in 1926, when the Chicago Board of Health imposed new, more stringent health regulations on dairy farms. However, dairying was still a significant part of Hanover life in the 1950s, even as farms were starting to give way to suburban development. Here, Art and Della Heine's daughters treat a young dairy calf to a drink.

By the mid-1950s, prime Hanover farmland was purchased by land speculators with an eye for potential suburban development. In 1956, 13 prefabricated houses sprang up at the intersection of Barrington and Schaumburg Roads. Many more small, ranch-style homes quickly followed in response to the post-World War II housing shortage. In 1957, the thriving agricultural community once known as Hoosier Grove was incorporated as Streamwood and became home to thousands of new suburban residents. Ontarioville was incorporated as Hanover Park in 1958. Bartlett evolved from a small town that served a farming region to a suburban village.

# *Two*

# GOING TO SCHOOL

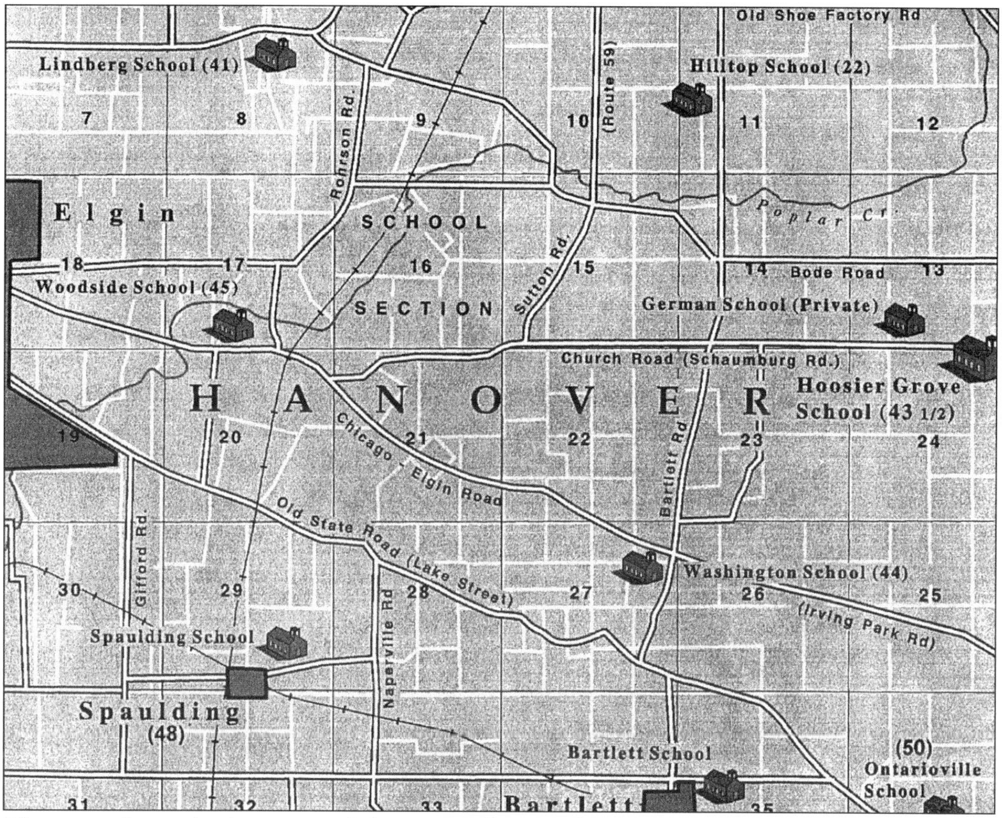


This map shows the locations of the nine village and country schools operating in Hanover Township before consolidation into U-46. It is a compilation of three maps dating from 1871, 1898, and 1920. Schools were designated by their district number and a name. Some names reflected a physical feature of the school's location (Hilltop and Woodside). Others honored famous Americans (Washington or Lindbergh). Names like New Era reflected a community's shared vision for the next generation.

Helberg School (later called Lindbergh School, #41) was located on the south side of Shoe Factory Road, one-half mile east of Rohrssen Road. Most likely, this was not the first school to serve the neighborhood. Maps indicate a school was located in this general vicinity as early as 1861. A brick schoolhouse was built on the Helberg farmstead in 1890, and was destroyed by fire in the late 1920s. Children temporarily attended school in a makeshift classroom located in John Tredup's garage. When the new cobblestone building was completed, the school was renamed Lindbergh in honor of the American hero of the era. Lindbergh School closed its doors in 1948 when District 41 was consolidated into Elgin School District U-46. Students transferred to Woodside School. At the time of this writing, several groups are trying to save Lindbergh School from the wrecking ball.

These children attended Helberg School in 1928. The first schools in Hanover Township were privately financed by subscription payments from parents or guardians of the pupils. The enabling act providing for Illinois statehood specified that proceeds from the sale of land in the 16th section in each township be set aside for the support of schools. When the first funds from this source became available in March 1843, residents met and divided the township into four rectangular school districts.

This Spaulding School class met in 1948. Unlike the majority of country and village schools in Hanover, Spaulding School served an ethnically diverse student population. Some of the students were German Americans from nearby farms, while others were members of railroad workers' families, who were often Italian or Irish.

Spaulding School (#48) was located on the north side of Spaulding Road, about one-half mile east of Naperville Road. Public education was prized by the immigrants who populated Hanover Township. Back in the "Old Country," education was for the elite classes, not the common worker. Public schools provided the basic reading, writing, and arithmetic skills that were useful in farm life.

Woodside School (#45) was located on the north side of Route 19, just east of the Lovell Road intersection. Although not visible in this 1934 photograph, a sign hangs above the front door. It reads "Standard School" and indicates that Woodside had successfully participated in the State of Illinois effort to upgrade and certify the older one-room schools. The following criteria for earning the designation was spelled out in the 1912 document "The One Room and Village School," published by the Office of Public Instruction: "the grounds, house, furnishings, heating, ventilation, library, water supply, outhouse, qualifications of the teacher, teaching and conduct of a good school are found present, a diploma will be granted designating it as a Standard School. A plate bearing the words 'Standard School' or 'Superior School' will be placed above the door."

Hilltop School (#42), shown here c. 1900, was located on the west side of Bartlett Road, one-half mile north of Route 58.

Hilltop School students pose *c.* 1900. Public schools were established to serve first through eighth grades. There was no kindergarten and few students continued on to high school.

The one-room Washington School (#44), shown here in 1932, was located at the southwest corner of Route 19 and Bartlett Road. Although the curriculum focused on basic skills, students learned other lessons and values that followed them throughout life, as reflected in this excerpt from a letter written by Warren Volkening to his Washington School teacher, Grayce Lamprecht: "I can remember the ball games we used to have, boys against the girls with you (the teacher) either playing or being the umpire. I can remember the tilt-a-whirl at the back of the lot. The boys and girls outdoor toilets that used to get knocked over at Halloween . . . [I] especially remember the small glass door library at the back of the school where I met Zane Grey and Dr. Dolittle. I learned to love books at that school and to this day I can't pass a book shop without going in to see what is interesting."

The original Bartlett School was built at Hickory and West North Avenue to serve the village children. In the early years, use fluctuated from one and three rooms depending on the size of the student body. Several additions were constructed over the decades.

This class posed at Bartlett School in 1908.

Another Bartlett School class can be seen in this *c.* 1910 photograph. The identification sign reads "Room 1," indicating that more than one room was in use at this time.

This photograph shows Irene Kelly Schultz's class at Bartlett School, *c.* 1921. Irene boarded with the Schultz family and eventually married into the family.

In 1915, a township-wide referendum to support the establishment of a high school was defeated. Bartlett citizens favored the creation of a high school and used public funds to establish a two-year high school in the 1920s. The high school met in the Bartlett School building. This photograph shows a high school class with Superintendent of Cook County Schools Dallas Puffer standing at the back of the room.

This high school class picture was taken in 1940, the year the high school closed.

The first site of Ontarioville School, shown here in the early 1900s, was one mile west of town on Lake Street just east of the Kenneke farm. It was a small frame building and was also used for church services on Sunday.

Ontarioville students pose for an end-of-the-year photograph at the original schoolhouse on Lake Street, *c.* 1912.

School Directors of District No. 50

F. C. Kaiser, President — Wm. H. Meyer, Clerk

Jake Nesler

Edward J. Tobin, Cook Co. Sup't of Schools — Lewis V. Morgan, Du Page Co. Sup't of Schools

Noble J. Puffer, Director of Education — Ruth A. Rathman, Teacher

Norling, Alstrom & Eckert - Architects

Pupils

| | |
|---|---|
| Roy Anderson | Velda Laue |
| Richard Andresen | Edna Marcy |
| Esther Bender | Helen Ruth Pierce |
| Lucille Bender | Donald Rinne |
| Marie Bender | Dorothy Rinne |
| Dorothy Cone | Eleanore Rinne |
| Clyde Feuerhaken | Arthur Schlueter |
| Ray Feuerhaken | Wallace Straub |
| Richard Fredricks | Robert Swihart |
| Harold Hitzeman | Anna Tilche |
| Albert Jensen | Frances Totenhagen |
| Elsie Jensen | Marie Totenhagen |
| Gustav Jensen | Elizabeth Wichert |
| Malinda Jensen | Lucille Wichert |
| Pearl Kenneke | |

# Dedication Program

of

## Ontarioville Public School

Ontarioville, Illinois

Wednesday, December 5th, 1928

In 1888, a new school was built in the village. This structure served the community until it was replaced by a modern two-room school in 1928. The new building is pictured here on the program from the dedication ceremony.

Hoosier Grove School (#43 1/2) was located on the southwest corner of Barrington and Church Roads on a corner of the Schuenemann farm. The one-half designation is said to be derived from the school's location on the border of Hanover and Schaumburg Townships.

This 1905 Hoosier Grove class had the good fortune to attend a brand-new school. Built in 1904, Hoosier Grove School served the community until 1954. It was the last country school operating in Hanover Township, and was replaced by the modern Hanover Countryside School.

Today, the Hoosier Grove School serves as Streamwood's community museum. The building was moved to Hoosier Grove Park in 1988. This photo was taken in 1914 with teacher Fred Martin.

Another Hoosier Grove School class can be seen in this *c.* 1938 photograph.

Art, Mildred, and Elsie Heine walked to school in 1918, as did most children. Contrary to tales of hardship recounted by generations of parents, schools were seldom more than a few minutes' walk from home.

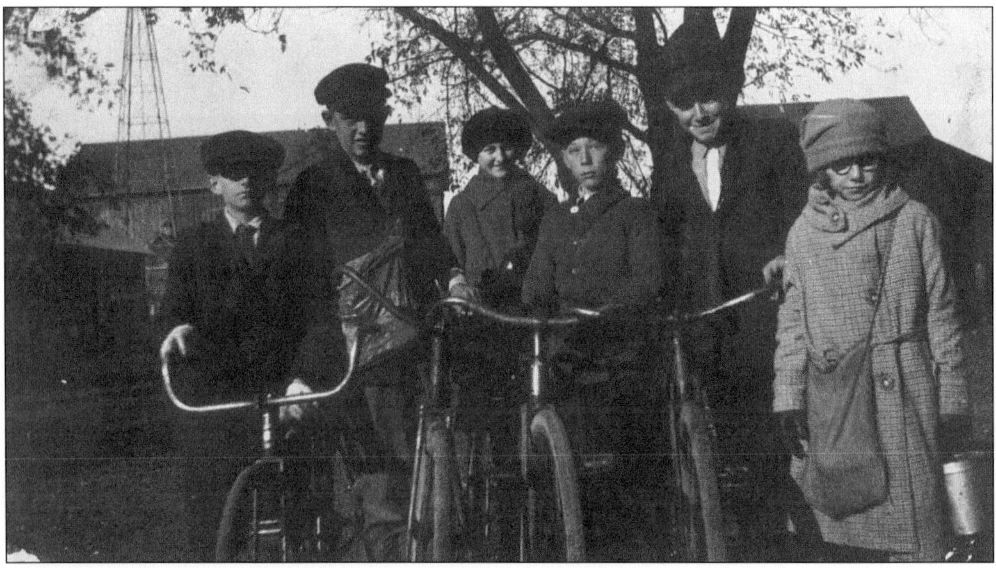

Hanover children also traveled to school on bicycle, *c*. 1925.

These children carried their lunch to school in pails. A typical lunch might include home-baked bread, sliced meats and cheeses, apples, and homemade pickles. Hanover children were well-fed by the abundance of food grown on the family farms. The lack of refrigeration made milk impractical as a lunchtime beverage. Children commonly carried flasks of sugar-sweetened coffee and placed them by the woodstove, where they were kept warm until lunchtime.

Schools, along with churches, served as the social center of the community. In the days before television, multiplex movie theaters, and shopping malls, evening events at the schools were plentiful and well attended. Special programs produced by the students and teachers were featured throughout the year. This photograph shows Hoosier Grove students dressed for a spring program, c. 1926.

Competition took many forms at the village and country schools. Students from throughout Hanover Township came together to compete in a spelling bee each year. Loretta Heine of Hoosier Grove School proudly displays a banner won at the 1928 Hanover Township Spelling Bee.

Arbor Day was celebrated throughout Hanover since it was first observed in Illinois in 1887. The day was devoted to tree- and bird-related study as mandated by state law. Students also donned costumes, marched, presented orations, and sang songs expressing the virtues of trees and birds at Arbor Day pageants held at the country and village schools. This photograph was taken *c.* 1916.

This township winner represented Hanover at the Cook County Spelling Bee held in Chicago. Irene Schramm of Woodside School displays the banner won at the 1939 Hanover Township Spelling Bee. Ms. Schramm is wearing a medal she won for taking second place at the Cook County Spelling Bee.

The Schramm family car was decorated to transport Woodside School students to the Beverly Lake festival in the spring of 1928.

Students from each of the Hanover Township schools competed each year in a variety of festivals held in Bartlett and Beverly Lake. Here, students from Woodside School display a first place banner for winning the athletic events on May 24, 1928.

Helberg students display banners won in a milking competition at the Beverly Lake festival in 1924. The school took top honors in both the dairymaids (students) and matrons (parents) divisions. This photograph was taken at Lord's Park at the end-of-the-year picnic.

These Hanover students participated in a celebration, *c.* 1916. The patriotic flavor of the costumes would have been common in the World War I era, when citizens, especially German Americans, wanted to make visible their patriotism and loyalty to the U.S.

Parents played an important role in the operation of the country schools. They served as trustees and were responsible for hiring and firing teachers. They also provided wood and coal to fuel the pot-bellied stove and made sure the building was well maintained. Pictured with buckets and scrub brushes, this group of mothers from Hoosier Grove School gave the schoolhouse a thorough spring cleaning in May 1939.

Parents sometimes organized special outings for the teachers and students to enjoy. Here, Hoosier Grove students enjoy "Mother Volkening's picnic." The spring picnic featured layer cake, homemade sandwiches, and a centerpiece of fresh-picked wildflowers, *c.* 1905.

The outdoors played an important part in the country school day. Fresh air, then as now, was thought to benefit the general health and well being of growing children. Some outdoor projects were designed to teach students skills they would use in their adult life. Here, Hoosier Grove School students Claire and Elsie Heine show off vegetables grown for a school project.

This photograph shows Hoosier Grove School students enjoying a snow fort built behind the schoolhouse, *c*. 1912.

The Heine girls enjoyed gathering wildflowers in the spring of 1927 for a May Day (May First) celebration at Hoosier Grove School. Fields and woods adjacent to most country schools made perfect surroundings for nature study. Walter Krog recalls how May Day was celebrated in 1914: "All the kids would take a walk to the woods. Then we'd pick different flowers . . . violets, the ones we called nosebleeds, bluebells, and different things." Back at the schoolhouse, the specimens were identified and studied, and then brought home as presents for mothers.

Country schoolchildren participated in organizations geared toward helping them learn skills they would need in adult life. Carol Blume participated in the Barrington chapter of the 4H Club. Her sewing project won a blue ribbon c. 1954.

The Cook County Achievement Club was a popular after-school activity. The club manual, from which this page is reprinted, outlined suggested activities for leaders to initiate in the following categories: Character Growth, Health, Civic Contributions, Library Readings, Agriculture, Hobbies, Fine Arts, Home Economics, Business Enterprises, Distinguished Service, and Punctuality. "Learn to do by doing" was the club's motto.

PLEDGE OF ALLEGIANCE TO THE FLAG

★

I pledge allegiance to the flag of the United States of America, and to the republic, for which it stands; one nation indivisible, with liberty and justice for all

★

COOK COUNTY YELL

C-O-O-K C-O-O-K

COOK COUNTY

Y-E-A

★

*"Learn to do by doing"*

(13)

The Cook County Achievement Club had its own song, reprinted here from the club manual, c. 1932. The lyrics read, in part, "We're the coming generation with a vit'lized education of Cook County in the State of Illinois."

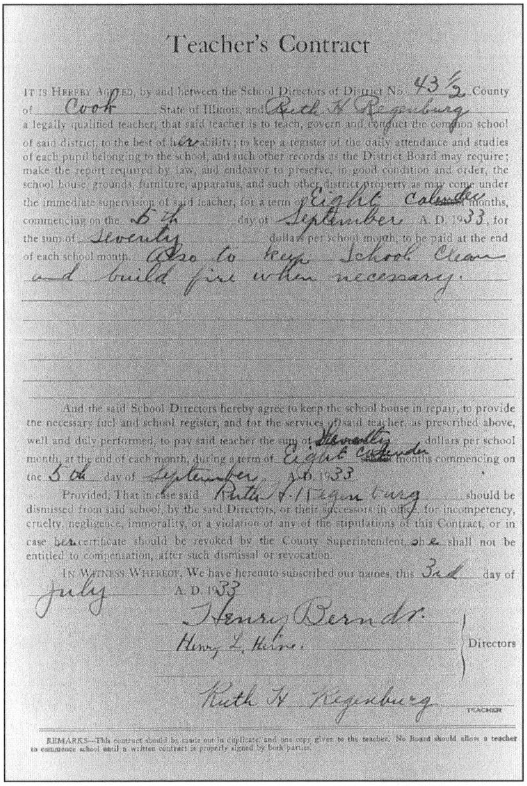

## Teacher's Contract

IT IS HEREBY AGREED, by and between the School Directors of District No 43½ County of Cook State of Illinois, and Ruth H Regenburg a legally qualified teacher, that said teacher is to teach, govern and conduct the common school of said district, to the best of her ability; to keep a register of the daily attendance and studies of each pupil belonging to the school, and such other records as the District Board may require; make the report required by law, and endeavor to preserve, in good condition and order, the school house, grounds, furniture, apparatus, and such other district property as may come under the immediate supervision of said teacher, for a term of Eight Calendar months, commencing on the 5th day of September A. D. 1933, for the sum of Seventy dollars per school month, to be paid at the end of each school month. Also to keep School Clean and build fire when necessary.

And the said School Directors hereby agree to keep the school house in repair, to provide the necessary fuel and school register, and for the services of said teacher, as prescribed above, well and duly performed, to pay said teacher the sum of Seventy dollars per school month, at the end of each month, during a term of Eight Calendar months commencing on the 5th day of September A. D. 1933.

Provided, That in case said Ruth H. Regenburg should be dismissed from said school, by the said Directors, or their successors in office, for incompetency, cruelty, negligence, immorality, or a violation of any of the stipulations of this Contract, or in case her certificate should be revoked by the County Superintendent, she shall not be entitled to compensation, after such dismissal or revocation.

IN WITNESS WHEREOF, We have hereunto subscribed our names, this 3rd day of July A. D. 1933

Henry Berndt
Henry L. Heine
Directors

Ruth H Regenburg
TEACHER

REMARKS—This contract should be made out in duplicate and one copy given to the teacher. No Board should allow a teacher to commence school until a written contract is properly signed by both parties.

Hanover Township issued its first teaching certificate to Miss Harriet Ballard in January 1843. Records documenting the lives of the early teachers have not been located. Most likely those charged with the responsibility of educating the children of pioneers were young men and women with little or no formal training. By the 1890s, most teachers serving various township districts attended one of Illinois' Normal Schools. The Normal Schools provided training and degrees for teachers in two- and four-year programs.

The 1932 contract at left belonged to Ruth Regenberg Anderson. Not only did it require her to teach all eight grades, but "also to keep [the] school clean and build a fire when necessary."

Ruth Regenberg Andersen and her pupils posed for a picture at Hoosier Grove School in 1934. Mrs. Anderson also taught at Spaulding School. Teachers played an important role in a child's life, as reflected in this excerpt of a letter to Mrs. Anderson: For me as for many others to recall the days spent in the schoolhouse is to recall many happy memories at a time when learning the right thing is so important to a child . . . School was sort of a home for all of us. No matter what kind of problem you had you could always tell the teacher and she would help you solve it. In my opinion, to be your kind of teacher is a wonderful gift too often missing today."

Teachers often came from towns too far away for daily commuting, including Chicago. They would arrive by train or be dropped off by family members on Sunday night, board with a nearby farm family all week, and head back home on the weekend. Ann Fagan, a teacher at Washington School, boarded at the Hecht farm.

Elvina Brandt taught at Bartlett School in the 1920s.

Helberg School teacher Mary Mason Beverly created handmade photograph souvenir booklets for each of her students. She took photographs throughout the year, wrote captions, and presented the mementos to her students as end-of-the-year presents. This photograph was called "Where we have oceans of fun," in the 1924 booklet.

Mrs. Beverly called this photograph "Just us girls."

This photograph was captioned "All here—excepting three."

"All aboard for a slide" was the caption under this photograph.

This Berndt family photo shows the children preparing to take the family tractor out to the fields. The school day ended around three in the afternoon, allowing plenty of time for play and chores before supper.

In 1958, even as suburbia cropped up around her family's farm, Mary Jane Blume was a typical farmer's daughter, comfortable on a tractor and ready to pitch in and help with chores.

Esther and Mildred Heine, Loretta Harz, and Harvey Bierman enjoy each other's company while hard at work in a farm field. The school year followed the rhythm of agriculture, with a long summer break to allow children to help out on the farm during the harvest. Modern schools still follow a similar schedule, even though the needs of the farm are no longer relevant to most students' lives.

CLASS ROLL

District 41 .......................... Teacher, Anne Fox
Marjorie Tredup — Albert Helberg, Jr.

District 42 .................. Teacher, Irene Lamprecht
Flora Meyer — William Feldman

District 43 .................. Teacher, Mabel Hinneberg
Pearl Nagel

District 43½ .................. Teacher, Ruth Regenburg
Edward Stumpf — Albert Behrens
Alvin Hecht — Florence Berndt
Phyllis Berndt — Ruth Heine

District 44 .................. Teacher, Grace Timmerman
Marion Alm — Leslie Sedenberg

District 45 .................. Teacher, Katharine Ostdick
Frances Landwehr — Mildred Nohl
LeRoy Schramm — Clfford Wenzel
Earl Schultz

District 48 .................. Teacher, Mary Blizek
Daniel Sylva — John Schroeder

District 49 .................. Teachers: Elvina Brandt, Eva Kampmeyer, Ruth Baxman
Lenora Knaak — Agatha Pleasant
Ruth LaRue — Lois Schmalbeck
Russell O'Brien — Ora Schick
Evelyn Schnell

District 50 .................. Teacher, Leota Phelps
Pearl Kenneke — Richard Fredericks
Arthur Schlueter — Frances Totenhagen
Eleanore Rinne

Director of Education .................. Paul J. Sheehan

PROGRAM

Invocation ........ Rev. Wm. Rathman, Bartlett
Class Introduction .............. Lenora Knaak
Salutatory .................. Marjorie Tredup
Piano Solo ................ Richard Fredericks
Class Prophecy ................ Pearl Kenneke
"The Old Water Mill" .......... District 43½
Valedictory ............... Frances Landwehr
Class Will ...................... Flora Meyer
Piano Solo .................. Russell O'Brien
Class Poem ..................... Marion Alm
"Graduation Song" ............ Class of 1934
Address ........ Rev. Alexander Milmine, Elgin
Presentation of Diplomas ...... Paul J. Sheehan
Response ....................... Pearl Nagel
Orchestra ...................... District 48
Remarks ...................... Tella B. Mills
Principal, Bartlett School
Benediction ............... Rev. Wm Rathman

For many years, all the Hanover schools came together in Bartlett for graduation ceremonies. For most Hanover students, eighth grade graduation marked the end of formal education. The closest high school was in Elgin, although a few students from the north end of the township attended Barrington High School. The commute to the high school, the lack of a bus service, and the cost of tuition and books kept most students home, not to mention the fact that their labor was needed on the farm. Most of the students attending the country schools were expected to become farmers like their parents; eight years of education was thought adequate to become a responsible citizen of the agricultural community.

Mildred Heine graduated from Hoosier Grove School in 1926.

COMMON SCHOOL
DIPLOMA
FOR COOK CO. ILLINOIS.

THIS CERTIFIES, that Laura Schuenemann of District No. 43½ Township No. 41 Range No. 9 County of Cook has completed the Course of Study in the Common Branches required by Law for admission to High School, viz:

Orthography, Reading, Writing, Arithmetic, English Grammar, Geography, Physiology, United States History.

In testimony whereof we have hereunto subscribed our names at Chicago this 13th day of June A.D. 1914

Opal Leah Helm
Principal

Edward J. Tobin
County Superintendent of Schools

A. H. Volkening
President of Board of Directors

Eugene M. Phillips

This diploma was issued to Laura Schuenemann from the Hoosier Grove School in 1914. Laura's parents donated property for the school building.

Eva Kampmeyer, a teacher at Bartlett School, is dressed in cap and gown for a graduation ceremony.

By the 1950s, the days of the one-room country schoolhouse were numbered. Seen here is a Washington School class, 1953.

This Hilltop School class was photographed in 1953.

This picture was taken at Hoosier Grove School in 1950.

The building of Hanover Countryside School in 1954 marked the end of the era of the one-room schoolhouse. The new building was quickly filled to capacity as the suburbs began to flourish. It was the last school built by the farming community. In 1955, all remaining independent country school were compelled to consolidate with Elgin School District U-46.

*Three*

# KEEPING THE FAITH

Church life played an important role in early Hanover Township. The three oldest existing churches in the township—all named Immanuel—were founded by the German families of the region. This photograph shows the Immanuel German Evangelical Church (now Immanuel United Church of Christ), founded in 1891 when members of the Immanuel Churches in Streamwood and Ontarioville wanted a church in their own community.

Immanuel was actually the second church in Bartlett. The first had been a Congregational church that began in the 1870s, meeting in members' homes and above a store. In 1879, a congregation in Wayne disbanded and gave their building to the Bartlett congregation. The building was moved that year to land donated by Luther Bartlett. The Congregational church, which was known locally as the "English church" as opposed to the "German church," was eventually razed and replaced by a savings and loan.

The carving over the altar in Immanuel Church, translated from German, reads "Glory to God in the Highest."

Originally, all Immanuel Church services were in German. These were switched to English during World War I, when anti-German sentiment ran high throughout the nation. Even German families who had been U.S. citizens for generations felt that their loyalty was under scrutiny during those tense years. Despite the discontinuation of German services, they were reinstated at some point. A church bulletin from 1939 makes a point of referring to the morning service as "English." These children attended a German parochial school affiliated with the Immanuel Church in Bartlett. The children received German language and heritage lessons as well as church instruction. German immigrant farmers were eager to keep their language and culture alive in the younger generation. Interest in German schools waned with the anti-foreign sentiments of World War I.

George and Ida Schick were the first couple to be married at Immanuel Church, Bartlett, in 1891.

This wedding photograph shows Carl Baumann and his bride, who were married at the Bartlett Immanuel Church. Baumann succeeded Gustav Hagemann as pastor of the church in the 1890s.

A later photograph of the Baumann family tells a sad tale. The portrait represents the deceased Mrs. Baumann.

Pastor Carl Baumann poses with a confirmation class of Immanuel Church, Bartlett, in the mid-1890s.

Along with the schoolhouse, the church building served as a central gathering place for the community. These ladies from Immanuel Church, Bartlett, posed for a photograph during a church function, possibly a picnic or meeting of the Frauen Verein (Ladies Aid).

Immanuel Church of Christ in Streamwood was organized in 1852 as the Deutsche Vereinigte-Evangelische Luterische Immanuels Gemeinde. Its founders represented a union of German Lutheran and Reformed congregations. In 1853, a building was constructed at what is now the intersection of Barrington and Old Church Roads. The present structure was built in 1869. Located in Hoosier Grove (now Streamwood), the church was commonly referred to as the Hoosier Grove Church, possibly to distinguish it from the other Immanuel churches in the area.

Dorothea Eleanor Friese was the first bride to be married at the Hoosier Grove Church. She married Ludwig Ernst Oltendorf on April 3, 1853; this photograph was taken later in her life. Like other early Hanover pioneers, the Oltendorfs immigrated to this country, in 1851, from Germany.

This photograph of the interior of the Hoosier Grove Church was taken *c.* 1895. Like the Bartlett church, it shows a German inscription of "Glory Be to God in the Highest" above the altar. The wood stove at the far right was used for heating the church.

The church played an important role in the development of Hanover children. Here, children of the Hoosier Grove Church are gathered with their minister in 1895 for a special occasion. The church was elaborately decorated for such events as confirmation, Easter, and Christmas.

The church's German school is on the far left. Children were expected to spend time in parochial school, where they would study religion and a general curriculum and prepare for their confirmation. At home, families sometimes spoke a mixture of German and English.

This class attended the German school of the Hoosier Grove Church in 1914. The school was built in 1879.

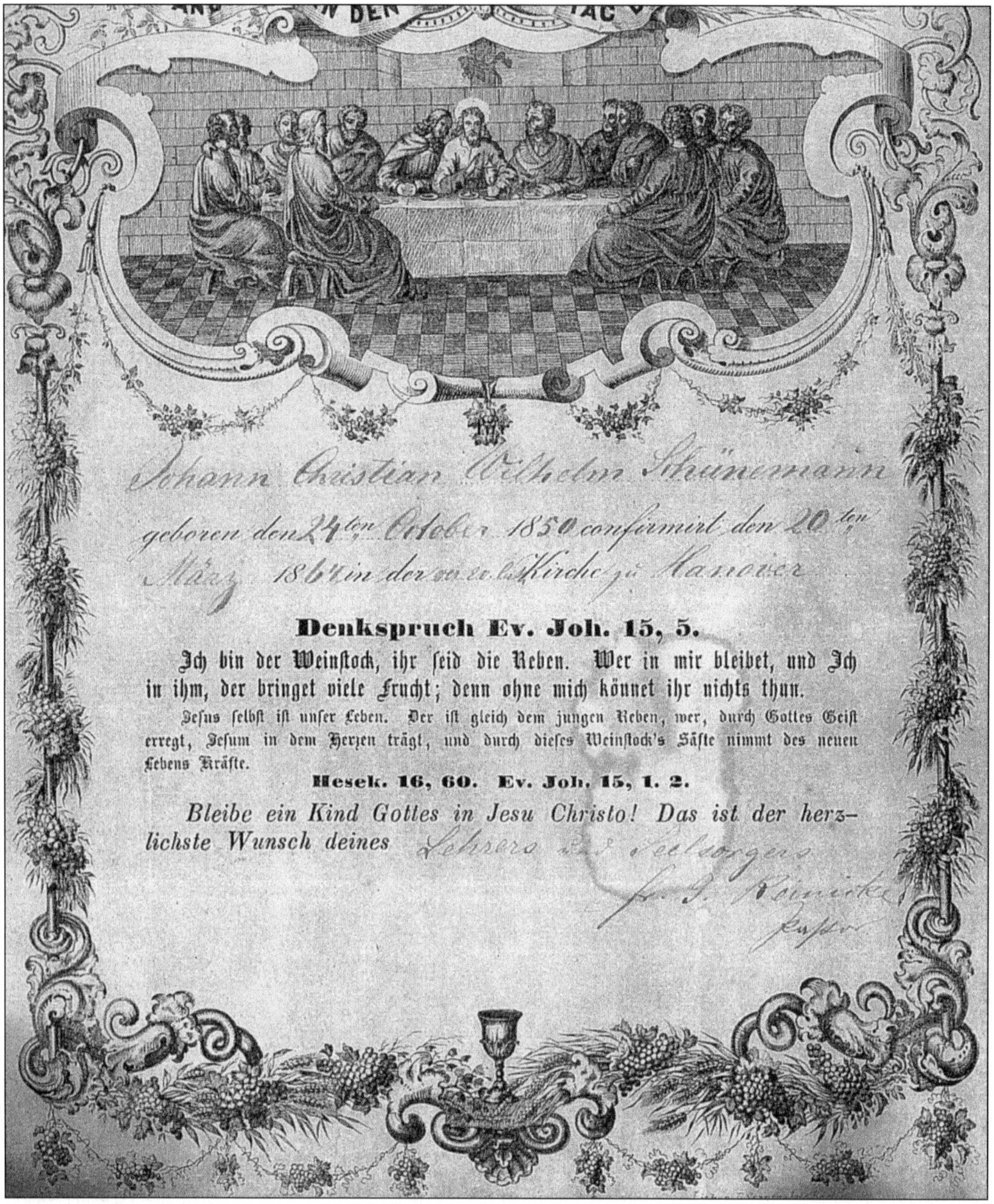

Johann Christian Wilhelm Schünemann

geboren den 24ten October 1850 confirmirt den 20ten März 1864 in der ev. luth. Kirche zu Hanover

**Denkspruch Ev. Joh. 15, 5.**

Ich bin der Weinstock, ihr seid die Reben. Wer in mir bleibet, und Ich in ihm, der bringet viele Frucht; denn ohne mich könnet ihr nichts thun.

Jesus selbst ist unser Leben. Der ist gleich dem jungen Reben, wer, durch Gottes Geist erregt, Jesum in dem Herzen trägt, und durch dieses Weinstock's Säfte nimmt des neuen Lebens Kräfte.

**Hesek. 16, 60. Ev. Joh. 15, 1. 2.**

*Bleibe ein Kind Gottes in Jesu Christo! Das ist der herzlichste Wunsch deines* Lehrers und Seelsorgers

Johann Christian Wilhelm Schünemann's 1867 confirmation certificate from the Hoosier Grove Immanuel Church reflects the German heritage of the community.

Confirmation was an important life passage in Hanover, as it signified adult membership in the church. Lydia and Amanda Flentge dressed quite fashionably for their confirmation at the Hoosier Grove Church at the turn of the 20th century. Girls typically wore white dresses for confirmation, while boys wore a suit and tie.

A local paper had this to say about a 1910 confirmation class: "Rev. Ellerbrake's class of 11 boys were publicly examined at Hoosier Grove church Sunday forenoon and will be confirmed Palm Sunday March 20. The class was smart in their examination and people enjoyed listening to their singing. They are Freddy Heine, Louis Humbracht, Harvey Tatge, Albert and Harry Flentge, Willie Toppel, Albert Dickman, Walter Sodt, Edwin Rinne, Herman Lamprecht, and Edward Krueckel."

A common practice was for the confirmation class to give a gift to the church. The 1910 class of Hoosier Grove Church gave this elaborate crèche, which was displayed at Christmas for years to come.

The 1926 confirmation class of the Hoosier Grove Church included the following, from left to right: (front row) Gert Rahlfs, Loretta Rahlfs, Melinda Hecht, Clara Hurske, and Laura Flentge; (back row) Harvey Bierman, Ray Hurske, George Thiess, Reverend Meyer, Fred Hartz, and Art Heine.

One Confirmation Day tradition was the confirmants' march from the Heine farm to the church. On Palm Sunday, 1926, the class appears to be buffeted by the wind.

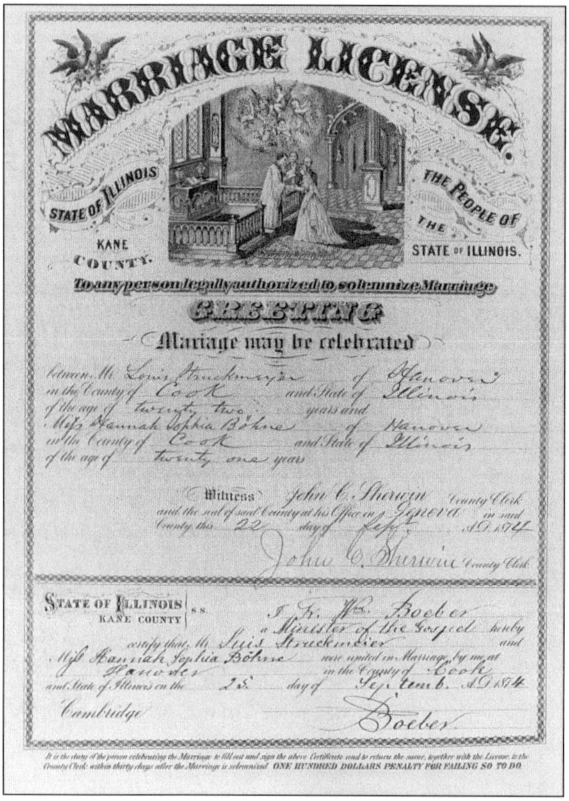

MARRIAGE LICENSE.

STATE OF ILLINOIS
KANE COUNTY.
THE PEOPLE OF THE STATE OF ILLINOIS.

To any person legally authorized to solemnize Marriage

GREETING

Marriage may be celebrated

between Mr. Louis Struckmeyer of Hanover in the County of Cook and State of Illinois of the age of twenty two years and Miss Hannah Sophia Böhne of Hanover in the County of Cook and State of Illinois of the age of twenty one years

Witness John C. Sherwin County Clerk and the seal of said County at his Office in Geneva in said County this 22 day of Sept. A.D. 1874

John C. Sherwin County Clerk

STATE OF ILLINOIS, KANE COUNTY } S.S.

I F. Wm. Boeber a Minister of the Gospel hereby certify that Mr. Luis Struckmeier and Miss Hannah Sophia Böhne were united in Marriage by me at Hanover in the County of Cook and State of Illinois on the 25 day of Septemb. A.D. 1874

Cambridge

Boeber

It is the duty of the person celebrating the Marriage to fill out and sign the above Certificate and to return the same, together with the License, to the County Clerk within thirty days after the Marriage is solemnized ONE HUNDRED DOLLARS PENALTY FOR FAILING SO TO DO.

This ornate marriage certificate commemorates the wedding of Louis Struckmeier and Hanna Sophia Böhne in 1894. The certificate was filed in Kane County, while the ceremony took place in Hanover Township (Cook County).

The wedding of Elsie Heine and Art Jahns was held on the Heine farm in 1929. Many of the Hanover families were related by blood or marriage, as the young people were likely to choose one of their childhood friends or someone who had grown up in a nearby township as a spouse.

Art Heine and Della Clausing were married on April 10, 1934, in the minister's house of the Hoosier Grove Church. The couple met at a barn dance, a popular social activity for young people. The Heines were a Hanover family. The Clausings had a farm in nearby Elk Grove. The wedding party included, from left to right, Emil Clausing, Arthur Clausing, Della Clausing Heine, Art Heine, Mary Heine, and William Heine.

Decorating the bridal car was as popular a custom then as now. Arthur Clausing posed next to the car after the 1934 Heine-Clausing wedding.

The Women's Guild of the Hoosier Grove Church was founded in 1911 to provide valuable services such as fund-raising, preparing food for celebrations, and calling on the sick. The guild provided an important social outlet for the women of the community. In the early years, they cleaned the church. This photograph is dated *c.* 1940.

In the absence of restaurants in Hanover, the church basement served as an assembly room and banquet hall. Here, Women's Guild members from the Immanuel Hoosier Grove Church stand ready to serve at the wedding reception of Junior and Gloria Radde, *c.* 1945.

Women's guild members dressed in old-fashioned clothes to present a play for the community, c. 1930.

The community gathered together in sad times as well as in happy ones. Given the geographic stability of farm families, multiple generations might be christened, confirmed, married, and buried at the same church. This is the cemetery of the Hoosier Grove Church.

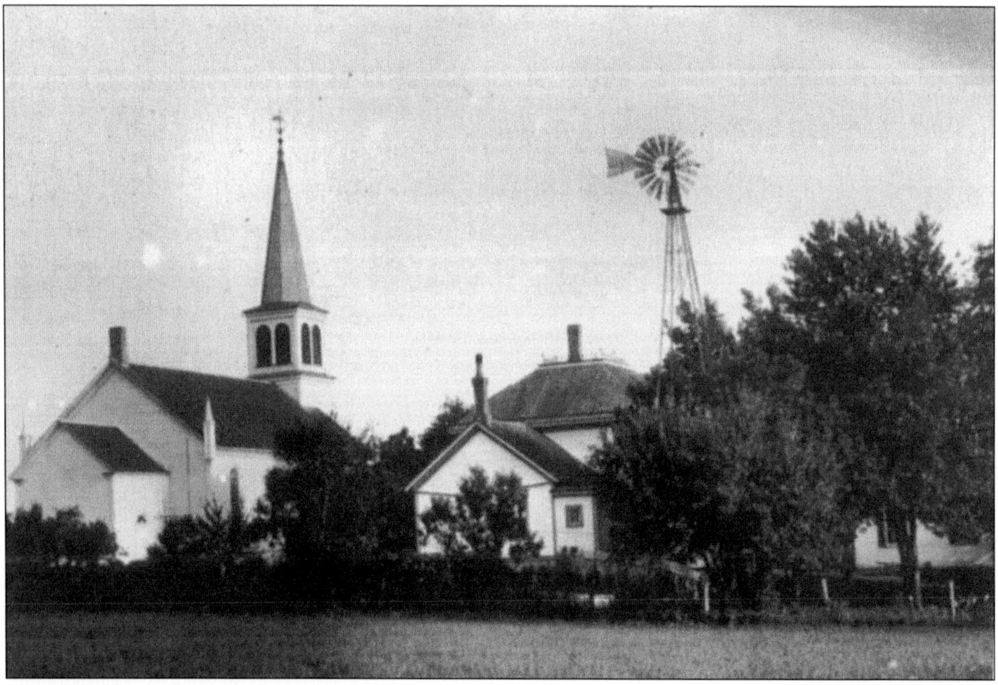

Here is a view of the church and parsonage from the cemetery, where many pioneers of the area are buried.

This photograph shows the funeral of Gustav Tatge, who passed away on August 27, 1910. The center floral arrangement features a sheaf of wheat to commemorate his life as a farmer. Gustav's son, Harvey Tatge, took on the responsibilities of the farm at age 15.

The Immanuel Evangelical Lutheran Church (Missouri Synod) was formed in 1899, but its congregation dates back earlier than that. Some of its original founders attended a church in Bloomingdale Township. In 1876, those members relocated to Ontarioville at the corner of Church and Ontarioville Roads. This building, which was rolled on logs to its present site, still exists and now houses the Smyrna Gospel Church. The Immanuel Evangelical Lutheran Congregation built a new church on Devon Avenue in Bartlett, *c.* 1964.

Early member rosters of Immanuel Church, Ontarioville, included the Schnadt, Leiseberg, Krumfuss, Feuerhaken, Koch, Scholer, and Harmening families. Some of these families helped found Immanuel Church, Bartlett, in the 1890s, when the need for a Bartlett-based church became apparent.

This class was confirmed at the Ontarioville Church, *c.* 1915.

Hanover Township remained an ethnically and theologically homogenous community until sub-urbanization in the 1950s. In 1929, a Lady of Victory Sodality was formed that led to the eventual founding of the St. Peter Damien Roman Catholic Church in 1949. With the influx of suburbanites came other churches, such as St. John the Evangelist, shown here, which was founded in 1962.

Other pre-1950 churches in rural Hanover are documented, but no pictorial evidence has been located by the authors. Included in this category is a church serving German evangelicals. The first services were said to be held on a log cabin on the Walbaum farm. All services were held in private homes in the winter and in Gellermans' Grove in the summer months. In 1861, a church building was erected on land donated by the Gellermans on North Bartlett Road. The cost of the building was $600, including the pews and a stove. This church thrived for many years. Some members later united with the Faith United Methodist Church. After the church disbanded, the building, which stood on the Gellerman farmstead, was used as a granary.

Camp meetings, held in summertime at Gellermans' Grove by the Evangelical Association, attracted large crowds. The first Methodist camp meetings were held in the Hoosier Grove area of Hanover Township, on the banks of Poplar Creek, beginning in 1839. These meetings continued well into the first quarter of the 20th century.

# *Four*

# Going to Town

A necessary part of farm work—and often a welcome diversion from it—was a trip into town. "Going to town" often meant carrying milk to train stations in Bartlett or Ontarioville for shipment to Chicago or to local dairies. Farmers would also head to Elgin or Barrington to load up on supplies. In this photograph, Mary Heine and a companion are setting off for Barrington in a horse and buggy. Mary was quite an accomplished horsewoman. Once, after a shopping trip, she drove from Elgin to Hoosier Grove in a record 30 minutes in order to reach home ahead of a thunderstorm.

These unidentified youngsters are all dressed up for a trip to town. Children were excited by a trip to town, which might include a visit to the candy store.

Seated *c.* 1900 on the steps of their parents' general store in Ontarioville are the Gieseke children. From left to right are Walter, Eleanor, Lillian, and Eddie.

This street scene in Ontarioville, *c.* 1900, shows Henry Gieseke and his horse, Bell.

Hanover farmers would have seen this view as they approached the Bartlett Train Station with their wagonload of dairy products, c. 1915. On Main Street (now Oak Avenue), looking south from North Avenue, they would have seen the telephone office; the tavern; the general store (later Eck's Tavern); a dry goods store with a barber in the basement; and the railroad station. All these buildings date from the 1870s.

Here's what the farmers would have seen if they left town heading north, on what is now Oak Street. The Leiseberg home is on the left; the park is on the right.

Railroad Avenue looking west from Oak Avenue shows the train station on the right and the tavern on the left.

Bob Charneskey was the station agent in the Bartlett Train Station in 1930.

This building housed Bartlett's general store, *c.* 1900.

If you were visiting Bartlett around the turn of the century, perhaps you would have visited Mr. and Mrs. Gustav Stumpf and their son Clarence at the northwest corner of Oneida Street and Oak Avenue.

The Krumfuss family is pictured here at their home at 120 South Oak Avenue. C.F. Krumfuss was a shoemaker.

This shoe and leather harness shop, run by the Krumfuss family, was located two lots south of their home on Oak Avenue. It was built in 1875.

A trip to town meant an opportunity to gather with friends as well as to take care of business. These young men are enjoying some "hanging around" time on a Bartlett Street in the 1920s.

In the early 1900s, a blacksmith shop was located near the present-day fire barn. Seen here, from left to right, are Otto Nimmrich, Herman Meyer, and an unidentified man. The blacksmith shop was a place to get needed repairs made, as well as to catch up on the news of the day.

This shop on Oak Avenue, south of the railroad tracks, has had many owners over the years. In the 1910s, when this picture was taken, it was the H.C. Thurnau Bakery and Sweet Shop.

A man named Diefer (left) and H.C. Thurnau appear ready to wait on customers in the sweet shop.

Farmers bringing their wares to Ontarioville *c.* 1900 would have seen this view of Devon Avenue; the Klazer house is on the right and the milk factory is in the background.

This *c.* 1900 photograph of Ontarioville shows the general store on the left. The store carried groceries, cigars, candy, dress goods, patent medicines, tools, hardware, and men's clothing. Sometimes, travelers stopping on their way between Chicago and Galena would be housed on the second floor of the store.

The general store also housed Ontarioville's post office for a time. Originally, the post office was in the train station. After some years in the general store, it was moved to the dairy co-op building. In the 1960s, the Ontarioville and Bartlett Post Offices merged.

A farmer stops by with a sleigh-load of milk cans in this photograph. Today, the building that was the general store in Ontarioville houses a law office.

Farmers brought grain to this Ontarioville gristmill to be processed. The gristmill, shown here in the 1970s, was built by Edwin Bartlett in 1876 and later owned by August Koch, a justice of the peace. It has since been razed.

Other structures in old Ontarioville included, from left to right, a blacksmith shop, the Scholer house, and a buggy shop. The Scholers owned the blacksmith and buggy shops. The buggies sold well, as farmers appreciated having an alternative to the farm wagon for non-farm purposes, such as courting.

Ed Scholer and his stepfather ran the blacksmith shop in Ontarioville.

# *Five*

# GATHERING TOGETHER

Farm work provided many reasons for Hanoverians to gather together. Friends, families, and neighbors met at farms throughout the area to assist with the hard work of the harvest. Men helped the hired crew in the fields while women busily prepared huge quantities of food for the midday dinner. Threshing day dinners included an assortment of farm-raised beef, pork, chicken, vegetables, and fresh-baked pies and cakes. The threshing day dinner captured in this photograph of the Tatge farm shows the women serving up a meal that would be long remembered by those present that day in 1920.

Fred Hecht's crew take a few moments to clown around while cleaning up equipment after threshing in the 1920s.

The threshing crews' wives and children were included in the end-of-the-year thresher's picnic at Rahlf's Woods, c. 1920.

After the threshing on all the Hanover farms was completed, Fred Hecht threw a big end-of-the-season party for his work crew and their families. The events were held at Rahlf's Woods, a local picnic grove located on the southeast corner of Route 19 and Bartlett Road. The day always included lots of beer, food, and family, friends, and neighbors. The music was provided by Herman Heine's Band (seated in front), which played at many events throughout Hanover. Fred Hecht is the large man wearing a full white apron just behind the beer barrel.

Other farm chores required neighbors to help one another. Sharing equipment and labor made for a somewhat lighter workload. Here, the Blume and Smith families are working together cutting and baling hay at the Blume farm, which was located in the general area where the Jewel Food Store stands today.

After the farm chores are completed, the Smiths and Blumes share a meal in the early 1950s.

Harvest time offered other opportunities to enjoy family and friends. Here, a group of Hanover women enjoy an apple harvest on the Tatge farm, *c.* 1915.

A new family arrives in the community. A young couple marries and receives a portion of the family land to establish their own farm. A storm or fire destroys an existing building. Whatever precipitated the need for a new building, a barn raising was always a community event. While professional "joiners" or carpenters were called in to oversee the project, farmers also relied on the manpower of family and friends. Follow these photographs taken at a barn raising on the Tatge farm in August 1927.

In this first photograph, a carpenter carries a piece of lumber to the barn building site. The main structural members, or bents, have already been assembled after many hours of planning and construction, usually by professionals called joiners. They are resting and readied on the main floor for raising.

A windlass, which will be used as an accessory in lifting the post-and-beam bents into place, straddles the end foundation wall. It assisted the builders in raising the massive structural members.

The first bent is raised into place by the barn builders. The large posts lock into the sill beams, which are secured to the top of the foundation wall.

The women sit on a lumber pile and watch the barn raising event unfold. Midday they would serve the crew a big meal, followed by another big meal when the barn was complete.

A toast is in order as the builders salute their progress. A Hanover custom called for a crew member to climb to the top of the building to "christen" its completion. The owner had to provide a wine glass for this ceremony, which, after being raised and toasted, was then smashed to the ground. The ropes are part of the pulley system that will be used to pull the next bent up in sequence.

With two more bents to erect, the framework of the barn takes shape. Once the framing was complete, the farmer and his family and friends usually finished the structure.

When all the bents were in their proper positions, siding would be nailed to both ends and walls. The rafters, roofing, doors, and windows were then all that remained to complete the barn.

This photograph of the Bartlett Cubs, a favorite area team, was taken in 1909. The Cubs played at a ballfield located on property owned by Herman Schnadt; the field is the present-day location of Bartlett Park. Organized baseball began in Hanover as early as 1871. The "Bluff City" team from nearby Elgin won a state championship in 1875. By 1920, almost every town and rural region had its own team. The Hanover Dodgers, the Bartlett Cubs, and a team from Ontarioville played weekly games against squads such as the Roselle Cardinals and Braves, the Dundee Bluebirds, the Elgin Monarchs, and the Elgin Nationals.

Hometown heroes like Walter Krog of the Hanover Dodgers entertained large crowds at weekly Sunday games. Krog posed for this photograph in his Hanover Dodgers uniform in 1928. Teams often purchased jerseys from big league clubs. From 1900 until 1940, amateur baseball was just as popular as professional baseball. On Saturdays, the *Elgin Courier-News* printed the line-ups for Sunday games. On Monday mornings, box scores and game accounts appeared on the front page of the sports section, along with the rundowns of the Chicago Cubs and White Sox games.

The team is pictured at Rahlf's Woods in 1923 before they got their professional-styled uniforms. Semi-pro teams purchased jerseys from professional clubs and sewed their own logos and lettering to create team uniforms.

A large crowd cheered on the Hanover Dodgers on a Sunday afternoon at Rahlf's Woods in 1930. Rahlf's Woods was located on the southeast corner of Irving Park Road and Bartlett Road and was home field for the Hanover Dodgers. Loyal fans enthusiastically rooted for young men who played for nothing more than the joy of hearing the cheers of fans and seeing their names printed in the local paper.

In addition to the weekly games, special tournaments were organized and played on summer holidays such as the Fourth of July and Memorial Day. Bartlett was the site of the annual Fourth of July tournament. The day was activity-packed and featured parades and orators. Members of local baseball teams can be seen marching in a Bartlett Fourth of July parade, *c.* 1920.

Parades have been a favorite amusement in the region for many years. In Hanover Township, most parades took place in downtown Bartlett. Residents from the village and surrounding farms gathered together for what we might now call old-fashioned fun. Here, World War I doughboys march in a parade in Bartlett. In the background is Thurnau's Sweet Shop.

Women and children carrying banners prepare to march in a Bartlett parade.

Herman Heine's band is carried by a decorated truck in this *c.* 1926 Bartlett parade. Heine, a hired hand on the Hecht farm, was the leader of one of the most popular groups in the rural portion of Hanover. German songs and polkas were heavily requested by his farming fans.

Hanover residents enjoyed good music and the area had many bands that played at community gatherings. Barn dances, parades, weddings, and funerals were all reasons to gather together and enjoy music with family, friends, and neighbors. This Hanover band played at a wedding held on the Harmening farm.

The German farmers loved their beer, especially after a hot summer baseball game or parade. Hanover men enjoy a tall, chilly one in the Bartlett Tavern, *c.* 1900.

Several young ladies catch a breath of fresh air on a beer hoist outside a Bartlett establishment, *c.* 1915.

Town wasn't the only place to enjoy a brew. A popular establishment was Grap's Tavern at Routes 19 and 59. The roadhouse was later known as Mueller's and it remained a popular gathering place through 1992, when it was torn down and replaced by a gas station.

Another place men liked to gather in rural Hanover was the Harz blacksmith shop, located at Buttermilk Crossing—the present-day location of Barrington Road between Routes 58 and 72. In the 1930s, a group of farmers belonging to the Pure Milk League (an organization similar to a union for dairy farmers) met at this location to discuss strike plans. In this *c.* 1930 photograph, the shop had been expanded to include auto supplies.

Weddings brought the community together to celebrate. This wedding took place on the Harmening farm (on Lake Street east of County Farm Road). The Harmening farm was the site of several elegant weddings. A local paper reported that one such wedding had over 1,000 guests at an outdoor reception. The railroad added extra cars to accommodate guests from Chicago. Dinner was served in the orchard and guests danced for hours.

Farmstead weddings were popular during the first decades of the 20th century, such as this 1927 wedding on the Flentge farm.

Times of sorrow and hardship also brought the community together. This photograph shows the wake of Herman Harz, a Hoosier Grove blacksmith, in the family's home. There were no funeral homes. Wakes were held at home and funerals were at either the home or the church. When a death took place, the church bells would toll once for each year of the deceased's life. This let the community know what had happened and called the people together. The bell was also used to signal other disasters, such as fires.

The community rallied together during all sorts of disasters. Those who lived in or close to Bartlett received the services of the volunteer fire department in case of fire. The group is pictured here with their new pumper. Bartlett's volunteer fire department in 1891 included, from left to right, Henry Harmening Jr., Ernest Schwake, Jake Schmidt, August C. Schick, Henry Waterman, George Struckman, Charles C. Schultz, Ralph Lobdell, Michael D. O'Brien, and A.C. Fisk. Henry Harmening is seated on the wagon with young William F. Harmening.

Those in rural areas had to depend on the help of their neighbors to fight fires. Without sophisticated equipment, the farmers had to rely on "bucket brigades" and the fires often won. The Heine family experienced a fire in 1927 and lost their entire home and its contents. While the house was being built, the family lived in one of the farm buildings. The community held a shower to help replace all that had been lost and offer their support in time of need.

At the shower, friends of the Heines offered not only material gifts but companionship as well. Good times could be had in the midst of trouble.

On July 3, 1933, a tornado devastated parts of Hanover. Many farmers lost their homes and barns. Once again, neighbors came to the aid of those who experienced losses in the tornado, offering shelter to both people and livestock and helping to rebuild the community. This photograph was taken on the Lamprecht farm. The men standing on a pile of hay where the barn once stood are WPA workers sent to assist the community with the cleanup.

These two unidentified women from Chicago paid a visit to the Struckmeier farm, *c.* 1905. Visiting was probably the most popular social custom. In 1910, a local paper ran a column called "Hanover Hurrahs," of which this entry is typical: "Mr. Ferdinand Lamprecht entertained company Sunday afternoon at which Rev. Ellerbrake and wife and Mr. and Mrs. Henry Helper, of Elgin and Mr. and Mrs. Herman Thies were guests." On Saturdays, women baked pies and coffee cakes and readied their houses for the anticipated Sunday guests. No formal invitation was needed; people always knew that they would be welcome in the homes of their friends.

This photograph shows a Sunday visit to Grandma's paid by Elsie and Clara Heine and their mother.

Many branches of the Struckmeier family are represented in this gathering, which typifies community life in Hanover Township in the early years of the 20th century. The farms and the fields of Hanover are no more. Yet on that rich soil flourished a community with deep roots and strong, generous branches. May the pages of this book serve as a reminder that for over 100 years, between 1850 and 1955, Hanover Township was a thriving, mostly German-American community where farming was a way of life.

# ACKNOWLEDGMENTS

This book is dedicated to the mostly anonymous photographers who captured images of a rural way of life that has nearly disappeared from modern-day Hanover Township, and to the many individuals who graciously donated photographs and mementos from their family albums to area historical societies. These keepsakes create a visual record of a vanishing way of life and provide new generations an opportunity to learn about their communities' pasts.

The authors also wish to thank individuals and organizations who helped create this book, including Pam Rohleder, the Bartlett Historical Society, and the Village of Bartlett, for photos from their collections; Janice Beckman, the Hanover Park Historical Society, and the Village of Hanover Park, for photos from their collections; the staff of Hanover Township, for making early records available; and a special acknowledgment to Mike Alft, author of *Hanover Township: Rural Past to Urban Present*. Alft's research and writing has contributed significantly to the preservation and understanding of Hanover Township's history.

Special recognition is extended to the Streamwood Historical Society and Streamwood Park District for providing the majority of images in this book from their collection, and for their extraordinary support and commitment to local history and preservation.